# A Walk in Nana's Garden

*I would like to acknowledge my parents,*

*Agnes and John Cruden, who have always*

*given me their full support, encouragement*

*and love in all my endeavours.*

*This book would not have been possible without the*

*curiosity of my granddaughter, Tilly, whose love of*

*the garden and its creatures inspired me to write.*

*Of course, I can't forget my loyal canine,*

*Ruby (Bee), who also loves the garden.*

# A Walk in Nana's Garden

Written by Fiona Lawley   Illustrations by Kerryn Lawley

A Walk in Nana's Garden
Author – Fiona Lawley

© Fiona Lawley 2022 (text)
© Kerryn Lawley 2022 (illustrations)

kflawley@gmail.com
www.adventureswithnana.com.au
P.O. Box 26, Maleny Q 4552

Illustrations by Kerryn Lawley
Editing, design and publishing support by www.AuthorSupportServices.com

ISBN: 9781922375179

**NATIONAL LIBRARY OF AUSTRALIA**

A catalogue record for this book is available from the National Library of Australia

Nana and I open the gate.

We walk into the garden and see what awaits.

There's a turkey sitting on his mound,

keeping his eggs safe and sound.

He likes to scratch the leaf litter around
as he searches for a snack.
But he keeps his eye on us as
we wander up the back.
He makes a little gobbling sound
to let us know he's watching.
"Don't go near my nest," he says.
"My eggs will soon be hatching."

There's a gazebo with a table and chairs,
where we sit and listen to the birds.
We can have a tea party, just Nana and me.
Oh, of course, we can't forget Bee.

There's an old iron tank filled
with water and plants.
Oh, look, there's some tadpoles.
Can you see?
They are feeding on the green algae.

There are bandicoots in Nana's garden.

They don't make a sound,

but you know they're around,

because they leave holes all over the ground.

Look at the kangaroos in the garden at the back.

They are very still, standing tall, no movement at all.

Suddenly, they hop away. It's not safe to stay.

We wave goodbye as they make their getaway.

Nana has many special trees

which mark the place

where pets now rest in peace and harmony.

Throughout the garden you can see

bird sculptures made from clay.

But if you want to see them all, it will take all day

Nana has trees which are very old.

She planted every one, so I am told.

Some are smooth and some are rough,

but each one is very tough.

They grow up high towards the sky,

where lots of birds are flying by.

Sitting in the gazebo, we hear a strange sound.
"Doo doo whip" comes from the
undergrowth and trees around.
What can it be? I can't see any birds around me.
"It's a whipbird," Nana says.
"He's looking for a mate."
"He's a shy fellow and isn't easily found. He's
hiding in the bushes and trees around."

We like to sit on the old woodpile and watch the cows next door.

Standing in the paddock, munching
away, is what they do all day.
The calves like to frolic and play.
Close to their mothers they always stay.

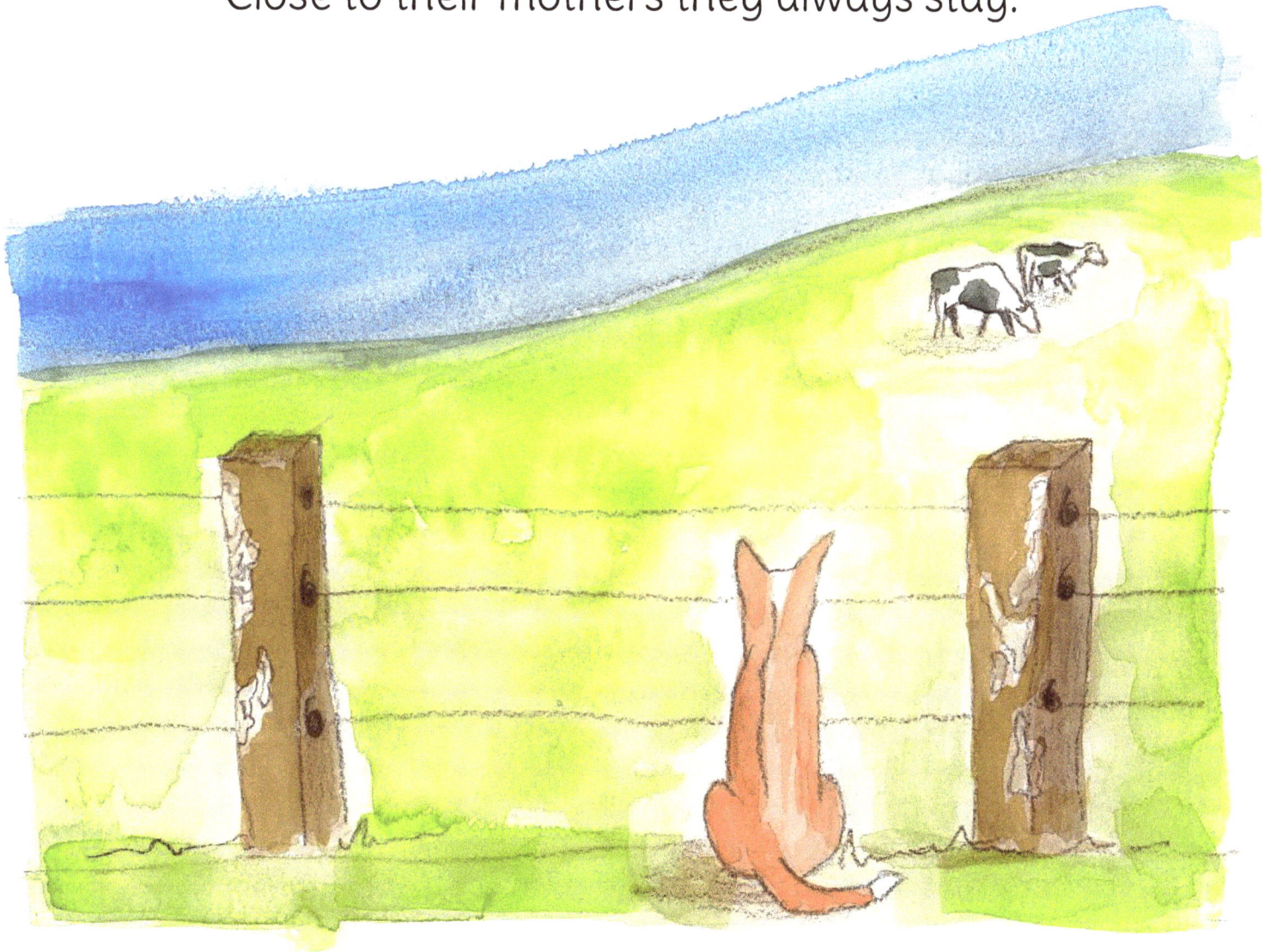

In the early morning and late in the afternoon,
the kookaburra choir like to sing.
Loud and strong they sing their song,
but it's not a friendly sound.
"Stay away from me," they sing.
"I don't want you around."

There are snakes in Nana's garden, but
they don't come out to play.
They like to hide in the bushes and hunt for their prey.
We often find discarded skins in trees or in the shed.
The snakes no longer need them so
they pull them off instead.
They grow a nice new shiny skin
which sparkles in the sun,
and they leave the old
one for us to find,
which is lots of fun.

Lizards like to lie in the sun to
keep their bodies warm.
But when they sense that we are
near, it fills them with fear.
All at once they seem to say,
"Let's run away from here."

We love to sit in the garden in the late afternoon.
The birds calling and flying in the
sky are a wonderful sight.
They're looking for somewhere
to sleep for the night.

The garden at night is an exciting place.

Stars sparkle in the sky and bats go flying by.

Possums dance in the trees above,

in the garden that we love.

## About the Author

Fiona and her husband live in Maleny. She has always enjoyed reading, and as a child, weekly visits to the library with her dad were a highlight. She has had several careers in office administration, childcare, teaching and aged care. Fiona enjoys spending time with her granddaughter Tilly and was inspired to write this book based on their adventures in the garden. Apart from engaging in the joy of nature, she enjoys pottery, reading, playing mahjong, yoga and walking with Ruby.

## About the Illustrator

Kerryn lives with her husband and their daughter Tilly in Maleny. She has been painting and drawing since she was a child. This is Kerryn's first professional project as an artist although she has always believed in creativity as an essential part of life. Kerryn works as an Occupational Therapist and counsellor and has recently begun to focus on her own garden, with Tilly's help of course.

For downloadable activities, books
and more, please visit me at

www.adventureswithnana.com.au

www.ingramcontent.com/pod-product-compliance
Lightning Source LLC
Chambersburg PA
CBHW042344030426
42335CB00030B/3448